Reinh

by United Library

https://campsite.bio/unitedlibrary

Table of Contents

Disclaimer

This biography book is a work of nonfiction based on the public life of a famous person. The author has used publicly available information to create this work. While the author has thoroughly researched the subject and attempted to depict it accurately, it is not meant to be an exhaustive study of the subject. The views expressed in this book are those of the author alone and do not necessarily reflect those of any organization associated with the subject. This book should not be taken as an endorsement, legal advice, or any other form of professional advice. This book was written for entertainment purposes only.

Introduction

 The book on Reinhard Heydrich delves into the chilling life and legacy of one of the Nazi regime's most sinister figures. As a high-ranking officer in the SS and German police, Heydrich played a central role in shaping the Holocaust, earning him the infamous title of chief architect of one of history's most horrific atrocities.

As head of the Reich Central Security Office and deputy Reichsprotektor of Bohemia and Moravia, Heydrich's influence extended throughout the Nazi apparatus. His chairmanship of the International Criminal Police Commission (ICPC) underlined his considerable impact, while his chairmanship of the Wannsee Conference in January 1942 formalized the genocidal "Final Solution to the Jewish Question".

Adolf Hitler himself nicknamed Heydrich "the man with the iron heart", reflecting the cruelty and brutality that characterized his tenure. As founder of the Sicherheitsdienst (SD), Heydrich orchestrated the suppression of resistance through arrests, deportations and murder, including the infamous Kristallnacht attacks. Directly responsible for the Einsatzgruppen, he oversaw the mass shootings and gassings of over two million people, including 1.3 million Jews.

The book also explores Heydrich's downfall through Operation Anthropoid, a daring mission carried out by Czech and Slovak soldiers trained by the British Office of Special Operations. Despite his death, Heydrich's malevolent impact endured, with Nazi reprisals targeting innocent villages, leaving a disturbing legacy that resonates throughout history.

Reinhard Heydrich

Reinhard Heydrich was a German *SS-Obergruppenführer*, responsible for Nazi war crimes and crimes against humanity. He was born on March 7, 1904 in Halle (Saxony) and died on June 4, 1942 in Prague (Protectorate of Bohemia-Moravia) from wounds sustained during an attack by the Czechoslovak resistance. At the time of his death, he was both Director of the Reichssicherheitshauptamt (RSHA) and Reich "vice-governor" in Bohemia-Moravia.

As Heinrich Himmler's direct deputy from 1933, he played a decisive role in organizing the Nazi repressive apparatus and eliminating the Sturmabteilung (SA) as a political force, mainly during the Night of the Long Knives in the summer of 1934.

He also played a major role in organizing the Holocaust, planning and controlling the activities of the Einsatzgruppen between 1939 and 1942, whose main mission in Eastern Europe was to exterminate Jews by shooting, and at the Wannsee Conference, which organized the logistics of the extermination centers and over which he presided on January 20, 1942.

Having unwisely chosen to be unprotected despite his rank, he was ambushed on May 27, 1942 by the

Czechoslovak resistance and the British Special Operations Executive. He was only slightly wounded by the explosion of a homemade bomb, recovered gradually, but finally died a week later, his condition having suddenly deteriorated due to an unexpected superinfection of his wounds. His death deprived the Hitler regime of a particularly effective leader; a man of great determination, he had been an essential link in the Nazi terror movement since 1931.

1904-1931: before joining the Nazi party

Reinhard Heydrich had an older sister, Maria (1901-1988), and a younger brother, Heinz (1905-1944).

His father, Richard Bruno Heydrich (en), was an excellent musician, graduating from the Royal Conservatory in Dresden in 1882 with the highest distinction; he went on to become a relatively well-known opera singer, notably at the Weimar opera, and later at the Cologne and Brunswick operas. A composer of some renown, he finally became director of the music conservatory in Halle, where Heydrich's mother, Elizabeth Krantz (1871-1946), taught piano and was inspector of the teacher training college.

His parents named him *Reinhard, Tristan* and *Eugen, Reinhard* after the hero of his father's opera *Amen, Tristan after* Richard Wagner's opera *Tristan and Isolde,* and *Eugen after* his maternal grandfather, Georg Eugen Krantz (de), professor of music and alderman of Dresden. From this musical family background came a lifelong passion for the violin.

In accordance with his mother's wishes, Reinhard Heydrich was baptized in the Catholic rite, while his father was a non-practicing Protestant. Like most middle-class people of his generation, his upbringing was strict and rigorous, in a nationalist atmosphere where absolute loyalty to the Kaiser was the rule. As he grew up, he became a resolute opponent of the Catholic Church, without however adhering to the neo-paganism dear to Himmler. Suspected of being Jewish, his father was the target of racist insults. The young Reinhard is shaken, his obsession with racial purity probably stemming from this trauma.

In his curriculum vitae written in 1903, Bruno Heydrich demonstrates a quest for honors and recognition that is shared by his son. In addition to his desire for recognition as a fighter pilot, Reinhard Heydrich collected titles far removed from his duties as head of the RSHA, such as director of the Fencing Office and Himmler's inspector for gymnastics; in 1940, he tried, unsuccessfully, to become president of the International Fencing Federation.

The end of the First World War with Germany's surrender on November 11, 1918 not only impoverished the Heydrichs and millions of other Germans, but also gave rise to the "stab in the back legend", according to which Communists and Jews had betrayed an undefeated army.

The Heydrich family was convinced of the truth of this theory, which was to become the basis for the commitment of future Nazis and numerous ultranationalist groups.

Early commitment

With the collapse of the German Empire, Germany was rocked by several left-wing uprisings, such as that led by the Spartakists, which were fiercely suppressed, often at the behest of the Ministry of Defense, Social Democrat Gustav Noske, by the Freikorps (free corps). Halle was also affected by the unrest.

In early 1919, a workers' and soldiers' council inspired by the Soviet model seized power in Halle. It was defeated by the Maercker Free Corps. After the end of the fighting, some of which took place near the conservatory, Heydrich joined the Freikorps Halle as a dispatch rider.

This early commitment was confirmed in 1920. The Kapp putsch, a reactionary attempt to re-establish the monarchy, was thwarted by a general strike organized by left-wing forces. The state of emergency proclaimed in Halle by Kapp's opponents was put down in bloodshed by government troops, even though they were rather close to the putschist, killing several hundred people. During this episode, Reinhard Heydrich enlisted once again, this time as a member of the Technical Rescue Service.

His involvement with the ultranationalist *völkisch* forces has sometimes been downplayed by his family, but there's no doubt about it. He was glorified by others, when in fact Heydrich held only insignificant positions - in 1919 after the fighting had ended, and in 1920 without taking part.

This commitment was both early and constant: in 1918, Heydrich joined a nationalist youth association, the *Deutsch-Nationaler Jugendbund*; he left it, then joined the *Deutscher Völkischer Schutz- und Trutzbund* in 1920. This organization, whose slogan is *Wir sind die Herren der Welt!* ("We are the masters of the world!"), aims to alert the German people to the threat posed by "the influence of Jews and foreign feelings and thoughts". In 1921, together with a friend, he founded the *Deutschvölkische Jugendschar*, an organization with which he kept in touch when he joined the Reichsmarine.

Heydrich completed his studies in 1922, with good marks. During this period, he became an accomplished sportsman, practicing swimming, running, sailing and fencing; as with the violin, his passion for sport persisted throughout his life. He became a world-class fencer and continued to take part in fencing competitions once he became head of the Reich's repressive apparatus. In 1941, he came fifth in the German fencing championships. In December of the same year, he won all three of his engagements against Hungarian fencers, while the German team was beaten by Hungary by a score of five to eleven, but these victories can be explained by his position as the powerful head of the Nazi repressive regime (the three Hungarian fencers would have let him win).

Brief career in the Navy

On March 30, 1922, he joined the Reichsmarine, no doubt influenced by his parents' friend Count Felix von Luckner's account of his campaigns.

During his military career, Heydrich was particularly noted for his sporting and musical talents, as well as for his female liaisons. In 1930, when he was promoted to ensign, he was ranked 23rd. After his promotion, he was assigned to the naval intelligence service in Kiel.

There were few highlights during these years, apart from the relationship established with Wilhelm Canaris, future Admiral and future head of the Abwehr, the military counter-espionage service. The good relations forged between the two men did not prevent the SD and Abwehr, and their respective chiefs, from waging a fierce war for control of the spy services. This conflict ended to the advantage of the SS and SD after the disgrace and resignation of Canaris in February 1944.

Heydrich's naval career came to an abrupt end in 1931. After announcing his engagement to Lina von Osten, whom he married some time later, he was dragged before a court of honor presided over by the future Admiral Erich Raeder, following the complaint of a young girl who considered herself already engaged to Heydrich. The identity of the girl and the exact nature of her relationship with Heydrich remain unknown to this day.

In themselves, the facts were relatively minor and were not expected to have any major consequences. But during the trial, Heydrich showed himself to be smug and contemptuous, demonstrating bad faith and arrogance: the verdict resulted in a dismissal for unworthiness, made public on May 1, 1931.

This hypothesis is questioned by Peter Padfield, who does not, however, endorse Heydrich's belated justification that he was expelled from the Navy because of his Nazi sympathies. In Padfield's view, this was a staged plan by Canaris to facilitate Heydrich's entry into the Nazi Party's intelligence services.

In June 1931, Heydrich found himself without a job or career prospects.

1931-1939: serving the party

The rumor of Jewish origins

Heydrich's career in the SS and RSHA was peppered with rumors of his Jewish origins, which had no serious basis in fact, but were repeatedly raised by his rivals in the Nazi regime.

At the root of the rumor was the fact that Heydrich's paternal grandmother, Ernestine Lindner, had married a locksmith, Gustav Süss, in a second marriage after the death of her first husband, Carl Heydrich, whose surname was borne by Jews and non-Jews alike. All would have remained as it was if, in Hugo Riemann's dictionary of music, the author hadn't followed his father Bruno Heydrich's name with the surname Süss, thinking thus to reveal his supposed Jewish origin, encouraged in this by a face of romantic intellectual and artist which, according to Riemann, gave Heydrich's father "the Jewish air."

On June 22, 1932, a commission for the evaluation of racial origin, whose research was carried out at Heydrich's request, stated that "in view of the enclosed genealogical list, it appears that Reinhard Heydrich, Ensign 1st Class, relieved of his duties, is of German origin and has no colored or Jewish blood."

Despite its particularly shaky foundations, this rumor was certainly a source of concern for Heydrich, and perhaps a means of pressure that Himmler could use against him. Indeed, until 1940, he had to plead before the courts for various "racial slanders", although he was cleared each time. The doubts that beset him, more than the contempt of certain Nazi dignitaries in the know, caused him great suffering, but paradoxically strengthened his determination, and his commitment to Nazism, leading him to build up files on all the pundits of the regime, especially on those whose rumors related to the Jews existed (in particular the "uncertain genealogy" of Hitler and Himmler, and the private lives of Goebbels and Rosenberg).

Creation of the Sicherheitsdienst (SD)

On May 1, 1931, the very day his dismissal from the Reichsmarine was made public, Heydrich joined the Nazi Party, and less than a fortnight later, on the recommendation of Karl von Eberstein, he turned up at Heinrich Himmler's home while the latter was nursing a flu. Perhaps the illness was just a pretext to organize a discreet meeting, out of sight of the SA. Not only did Himmler accept him into the SS, whose selection criteria and discipline were much stricter than those of the SA, but he immediately entrusted him with the creation of the Nazi Party's intelligence service, the future Sicherheitsdienst (SD), based on his experience in the naval intelligence service in Kiel. Called the "Ic Service", its activities began in Munich on August 10, 1931, with non-existent resources and total amateurism.

This new service rapidly grew in strength, gathering intelligence first and foremost on police infiltrators and enemies of the Nazi party, but also and above all on members of the Nazi party and the SA. It also serves as an instrument of extortion to finance the expansion of the SS.

He joined the Nazi Party on June 1, 1931, under number 544 916, then the SS on July 14, 1931, with number 10120. Hard-working, a good organizer, a convinced Nazi and Himmler's direct deputy, Heydrich was promoted to *Hauptsturmführer* on December 1, 1931.

On December 26, 1931, Reinhard Heydrich married Lina von Osten (1911-1985) at the Evangelical Church of Sant Katherina in Großenbrode, in a wedding that abounded in Nazi symbols: as they entered, the bride and groom paraded between two rows of local Nazi notables performing the Hitler salute, the altar wall was decorated with a swastika and, at the end of the service, the organ played the *Horst-Wessel-Lied*. This decorum can only please the bride, whose entire family is Nazi, one of her cousins being the author of the proverb "On Fehmarn [the island in Holstein where Lina was born] there are no snakes, no moles and no Jews. "Four children will be born from this marriage:

- Klaus (born June 17, 1933, died October 24, 1943);

- Heider (born December 28, 1934);

- Silke (born April 9, 1939);

- Marte (born July 23, 1942).

As a wedding present, Himmler appoints Heydrich *Sturmbannführer*.

In July 1932, he was officially appointed head of the Sicherheitsdienst (SD), the new name for the Ic service, and again promoted, this time to the rank of *Standartenführer*.

On January 30, 1933, Hitler was appointed Reich Chancellor by President Paul von Hindenburg.

Heydrich promoted Hitler's appointment as Chancellor by implicating Hindenburg's son Oskar in the embezzlement of Osthilfe subsidies, intended to support agriculture in East Prussia, and by fabricating the threat of a communist coup attempt.

Heinrich Himmler took over as head of the Munich police force, and Heydrich became his deputy for the political section, while remaining head of the SD. He took part in the Nazi regime's first crackdowns in February, and helped to fill the Dachau camp, which opened in March 1933 and was handed over to the SS in April. To do this, he relied in particular on the *Reichstagsbrandverordnung*, the emergency ordinance for the protection of the people and the state, adopted the day after the Reichstag fire (in the preparation and execution of which he himself is said to have participated with the help of his brother Heinz, a well-informed journalist), which allowed fundamental freedoms and *habeas corpus to be* suspended.

Heydrich blocked all attempts at legal control over what happened inside the camp.

In a letter to the *Reichsstatthalter* of Bavaria, Franz von Epp, in June 1933, he demanded that Thomas Mann, winner of the Nobel Prize for Literature, be interned in Dachau as soon as he returned to Munich (Mann had left Germany by then), because he had, according to Heydrich, "an un-German stance, enemy of the national movement, Marxist and Judeophile". Failing this, his property and assets were seized.

We move from the street terror of the SA to the state terror of the SS, even if the latter is still officially subordinate to the SA.

Night of the Long Knives

In 1934, Heydrich, along with Heinrich Himmler, was one of the architects of the Night of the Long Knives, which led to the elimination of the SA as a political force and made the SS directly subordinate to the Führer. With over four million members totally devoted to its leader, Ernst Röhm, the SA demanded social and economic reforms; its desire to take control of the army aroused the opposition of the military leadership that Hitler so urgently needed.

Heydrich manages to convince Hitler of the existence of a plot hatched by Röhm, in reality dreamed up by himself, Himmler and Hermann Göring.

After repressive measures had been approved by Hitler, who was nevertheless reluctant to have Röhm executed, the SA was decapitated by Himmler and Heydrich's troops on the night of Friday June 29 to Saturday June 30, 1934, an operation which continued until Monday July 2. The detailed files patiently compiled by Heydrich and the SD since 1931 are particularly useful for identifying victims.

The purge claimed around a hundred victims, including Röhm, whose assassination was attributed to Michel Lippert, and Theodor Eicke (future concentration camp inspector, then commander of the 3 SS "Totenkopf" division). Numerous SA leaders were also executed, as were opponents of Hitler, both internal, such as Gregor

Strasser, during whose agony Heydrich shouted "let the pig bleed to death", and external, such as former Chancellor Schleicher. The list of executions was signed by Heydrich himself, who received the eighteen killers sent by Sepp Dietrich and designated their targets before the murders began. Some of the murders took place in the courtyard of Munich's Stadelheim prison, with the firing squad commanded by Sepp Dietrich himself.

It was at Heydrich's insistence that Erich Klausener, director of Catholic Action and an official in the Ministry of Transport, who had opposed the Nazis when he was police director in the Prussian Ministry of the Interior, was murdered. For Heydrich, an opponent of the Catholic Church, Klausener's statement that mass was a special recognition of the Church's social action, and his public preaching against the Nazis at the Catholic Action Day in Hoppergarten, were intolerable. Heydrich personally hands over a pistol to *Hauptsturmführer* Kurt Gildisch, with formal orders to shoot Klausener by his own hand. This time, Heydrich chose a personal victim, outside the scope of the SA and Party purge. For Hermann Göring, Klausener's murder "was a truly savage action by Heydrich".

Even Wilhelm Frick, a committed Nazi and Minister of the Interior, was shocked by Heydrich's cruelty. In May 1935, he declared that "I may later be forced to allow Himmler into the Ministry, but under no circumstances will the murderer Heydrich be admitted".

The SS thus eliminates a rival organization on which it is still formally dependent. In gratitude for his services, Heydrich is again promoted, this time to the rank of *Gruppenführer*.

Reichssicherheitshauptamt (RSHA)

When, in 1936, Heinrich Himmler became *Chief of the Deutschen Polizei* (head of all German police forces), after many struggles for influence, notably with Hermann Göring, Heydrich became his right-hand man.

When the Reichssicherheitshauptamt (known by its acronym RSHA) was created in 1939, Heydrich was promoted to the head of the new unit and from then on supervised :

- the Sicherheitsdienst (SD), an SS organization which he had headed since its creation in 1931, and which included the two operational units *SD-Inland* and *SD-Ausland*;

- and complemented by the Sicherheitspolizei (Sipo), a state organization combining the Gestapo and the Kriminalpolizei.

The heads of the RSHA's four main departments - Müller, personally chosen by Heydrich and confirmed in his post,

Nebe, Ohlendorf and Schellenberg - were present throughout the Nazi repression. Heydrich's four deputies, with their varied profiles, proved to be highly effective.

Müller, aged 36 in 1936, and Nebe, 42, were both professional policemen who had begun their careers in the early 1920s. Müller faithfully served the Weimar Republic, for which he hunted down Nazis and Communists alike; indeed, he only joined the NSDAP on May 31, 1939. Nebe, on the other hand, had been a party activist since 1931. Ohlendorf, 29, and Schellenberg, 26, have more intellectual profiles. Ohlendorf graduated in law and economics from the universities of Leipzig and Göttingen, while Schellenberg studied medicine and law at the University of Bonn. Ohlendorf had been a member of the NSDAP since 1925 and of the SS since 1926; Schellenberg only joined the party in 1933, shortly before he was recruited as a jurist at the Sicherheitsdienst.

The Gestapo, a political police force, was responsible for tracking down, interning and eliminating opponents, while the Kripo played the role of a traditional criminal police force.

One of the *SD-Inland*'s tasks is to report on the integration of the National Socialist worldview, the *Weltanschauung,* into the individual sphere, to determine whether there is opposition to it, and if so, to identify the opponents. The *SD-Ausland, in* addition to its classic espionage missions, draws up lists of personalities to be eliminated, notably in Austria, and elaborates "solutions to the Czech and Russian problems".

The only police force outside Heydrich's authority and directly subordinate to Himmler as *Chief of the Deutschen Polizei* was the Ordnungspolizei, the uniformed police force responsible for maintaining order in the classical sense of the term (gendarmerie, traffic police, urban and rural police, etc.), headed by Kurt Daluege.

From the moment of the Anschluss, the annexation of Austria to Germany on March 13, 1938, Heydrich, who had played an active part in its preparation, used his repressive tools against Austrian opponents with the same vigor he had deployed in Germany. After filling the Dachau concentration camp, it was now the turn of Mauthausen.

Since 1935, the SD has also had a new tool of repression at its disposal: preventive detention (*Schutzhaft), which* enables it to intern anyone it likes without any court proceedings, and which it uses extensively in Germany and all the occupied territories.

From December 7, 1941, the *Schutzhaft* was even more terrible, with the coming into force of the "Night and Fog" decree, which required prisoners to disappear without a trace and forbade them to give their relatives any information about their fate or whereabouts.

Crystal Night

On November 9, 1938, Heydrich was in Munich, where Hitler was celebrating the anniversary of the attempted seizure of power in the 1923 Brewery putsch, in the presence of Joseph Goebbels and numerous Nazi leaders.

After Hitler learned of the death of the diplomat Ernst vom Rath, murdered in Paris by Herschel Grynszpan, a young Polish Jew whose parents had been expelled from Germany during the *Polenaktion*, Goebbels gave a hate speech to the Nazi party leaders, calling for "spontaneous actions" in retaliation against the Jews, immediately relayed by the participants to their troops: pogroms were unleashed all over Germany. In fact, the spontaneous actions were a campaign orchestrated by the Nazi party and led by the SA, but without the swastika flags.

Although Heydrich did not initiate the outbreak of violence against the Jews and, according to some authors, disapproved of this savage outburst of violence, he was involved in supervising the operation and sent the following telegram:

"Only actions that do not endanger German life and property are to be carried out (e.g. burning synagogues only if there is no danger of them spreading). Jewish businesses and apartments will only be ransacked, not plundered".

- Reinhard Heydrich, on the night of November 9-10, 1938

A few hours later, he clarified that "actions against Jews were not to result in any sanctions".

On November 12, at an inter-ministerial conference, he again drew up the balance sheet of anti-Jewish actions: 7,500 stores and 177 synagogues destroyed, over one hundred million marks worth of damage, and 91 dead. At the same meeting, he proposed concentrating Jews in ghettos, making them wear a distinctive badge, and excluding them from public transport, hospitals, schools and all places where they might come into contact with Germans.

In addition to the official figures drawn up by Heydrich, some twenty thousand Jews were deported to concentration camps, thanks to collaboration between the political police and the ordinary police.

"Even if we completely eliminate the Jew from the economy, the fundamental problem remains: the Jew must leave Germany", said Reinhard Heydrich on November 12, 1938.

During his assessment, Heydrich also praised the merits of the central emigration office set up in Vienna in March

1938, for which he had put Adolf Eichmann in charge, and which had accelerated the departure of Jews, fifty thousand of whom had left Austria since the Anschluss. On January 24, 1939, this model was extended to the entire Reich, under the direct authority of Heydrich.

1939-1942: repression and extermination

The invasion of Poland

At the beginning of August 1939, at the request of Hitler and Himmler, Heydrich organized a staged attack on the German radio station at Gleiwitz and the customs post at Hochlinden on the night of August 31-September 1, 1939, which Hitler used as a pretext to invade Poland. "When the tanks roll, no one will talk about it anymore," says Reinhard Heydrich.

For Hochlinden, Heydrich orders the Gestapo to extract six deportees from the Sachsenhausen camp and execute them. Their corpses, dressed in Polish uniforms, were laid out around the customs post. The same technique is used at Gleiwitz.

The execution of these two operations was entrusted to the Gestapo, more specifically to Heinrich Müller and Alfred Naujocks. These two men also organized the Venlo incident, the kidnapping of two British secret agents in the Netherlands on the night of September 8-9, 1939.

On the morning of September 1, 1939, German troops crossed the border: the Polish campaign began.

Creation of the Einsatzgruppen

The creation of the Einsatzgruppen was clearly ideological and racial in nature, and represented the first stage in the destruction of Europe's Jews. During the Polish campaign, in the wake of the Wehrmacht, the Einsatzgruppen, formed in July by Reinhard Heydrich, proceeded with the planned massacre of the Polish elite, focusing on Jews considered potential opponents. From September 1939 to spring 1940, sixty thousand people were executed in what turned out to be the "first stage of the Polish Holocaust".

While the Wehrmacht also committed numerous exactions in retaliation for the actions of mostly imaginary snipers, thus initiating the process of "barbarization" of the German army, the actions of the Einsatzgruppen were planned even before the invasion began, and were directed at predefined victims, considered to be opponents or potential future opponents of the German occupation. As Heydrich put it: "We want to protect the little people, but the aristocrats, the curetons and the Jews must be eliminated".

In terms of the organization of the actions to be carried out, the lessons of the Einsatzgruppen's action in Poland were drawn on during the attack on the Soviet Union, in particular to avoid tensions with the Wehrmacht, some of whose officers had protested against the brutality of the SS in Poland. In the Soviet Union, the tasks and deployment zones of the Einsatzgruppen, as well as their mode of collaboration with the Wehrmacht, were defined in consultation with the highest military authorities, even before the start of operations.

Following written instructions from Heydrich on September 21, 1939, the concentration of Jews in ghettos in towns with rail links began at the end of September, and *Judenräte* (Jewish councils) were set up "to facilitate future measures".

In November and December 1939, eighty-seven thousand Jews and Poles were deported from the part of Poland annexed to the Reich to the "General Government", at the cost of incessant conflicts with its leader, Hans Frank. This experience would later be put to good use when action against the Jews was taken in Germany and all the occupied territories.

In December, Heydrich appointed Adolf Eichmann director of the Gestapo's special section IV B4, later to become *Amt* B4, to provide a specialist in the Jewish question.

Organizing the destruction of Europe's Jews

In 1939 and 1940, Heydrich studied the possibilities of emptying the Reich of all Jews: in particular, he entrusted Eichmann with the task of drawing up a plan to deport the entire Jewish population to the island of Madagascar. But as early as June 1940, he realized that the "Jewish question" could not be resolved by emigration. In March 1941, three months before the start of the invasion of the Soviet Union, Heydrich, with Hitler's agreement, contacted Hermann Göring to work out a solution to the "Jewish question".

In the months leading up to the invasion of the Soviet Union on June 22, 1941, Heydrich held intensive negotiations with army officials to better coordinate the Einsatzgruppen with military operations. Given the scale of the conflict ahead, the difficulties encountered in Poland could not be repeated. An agreement was finally reached to precisely define the missions of each party, but this did not prevent tensions and contradictions.

Four Einsatzgruppen were formed, two of which were headed by Heydrich's close associates: Arthur Nebe, head of Office V (Criminal Police or Kripo) for Group B, and Otto Ohlendorf, head of Office III (*SD-Ausland*) for Group D; Group A was headed by Franz Walter Stahlecker, Group C by Otto Rasch. Appointed by Heydrich without having volunteered, they carried out their tasks with formidable efficiency.

As in Poland, but on a much larger scale, the four groups swooped in on the German armies as soon as Operation *Barbarossa* began, systematically eliminating Communist Party cadres - especially if they were Jews - Red Army political commissars, partisans and suspected partisans, and those who sheltered and supported them or were suspected of doing so.

At the end of July 1941, the action was extended to all Jews, men, women and children. According to Walter Blume, head of Einsatzkommando 7a of Einsatzgruppe B, and Karl Jäger, head of Einsatzkommando 3 of Einsatzgruppe A, it was Heydrich who gave the order to execute the entire Jewish population.

It was no longer necessary to be a real or potential opponent: the mere fact of being a Jew was enough to be executed.

The most terrible massacre was carried out by Einsatzgruppe C at Babi Yar, near Kiev, on September 29 and 30, 1941, with almost 34,000 victims.

At the end of August or beginning of September, Heydrich confirms in a meeting with Eichmann that "the Führer has ordered the physical elimination of the Jews".

In order to speed up the extermination of the Jews, but also to spare the killers' nerves, the first gas trucks (already used in Germany for the extermination of the mentally ill, directed and executed by Heydrich's services) appeared on the Eastern Front in December 1941. On December 7, 1941, the first gassings took place at the Chełmno extermination center, the only camp administered by the Sipo. The other extermination and concentration camps did not come under Heydrich's authority, but under Himmler's, through the *Wirtschafts- und Verwaltungs-Hauptamt*, headed by Oswald Pohl.

Following the organization of the Einsatzgruppen, whose activities he never attended, but whose results he constantly monitored and whose reports he read every day, on July 31, 1941, Göring entrusted Heydrich with the task of "producing, as soon as possible, a comprehensive draft of the first practical organizational measures to be taken to bring about the much-desired solution of the Jewish problem". On the basis of this instruction, Heydrich organized the Wannsee Conference on January 20, 1942.

The fourteen participants, invited by Heydrich, were not high-profile officials and represented various ministries, the General Government, the party apparatus and the SS; among them were also Heydrich's men, including Heinrich Müller and Adolf Eichmann, the latter acting as conference secretary.

"Heydrich began by explaining the mission entrusted to him by the Reich Marshal [Göring] in preparation for the final solution of the Jewish question in Europe, and stated that the aim of the meeting was to clarify fundamental issues. The Reich Marshal's wish to be presented with a plan of organization, procedures and material conditions for the final solution of the Jewish question in Europe, required prior harmonization of all the central bodies directly concerned with these questions, with a view to a parallel direction of action".

He is also clear about the methods to be used: "During the Final Solution, the Jews of Eastern Europe will have to be mobilized for work with the appropriate supervision. In large columns of workers, separated by sex, the Jews fit for work will be brought in to build roads in these territories. This will undoubtedly lead to a substantial natural decrease in their numbers."

Finally, appropriate treatment will have to be applied to all those who remain, since they will obviously be the most resistant elements, since they are the result of natural selection, and could be the seeds of a new Jewish strain, if left to their own devices (see the experience of history)."

For Heydrich, it was no longer just a question of applying the Final Solution, the *Endlösung*, to the Jews of the Reich alone, but of extending it to all the Jews of Europe, whose number he estimated at 11 million.

The conference lasted barely two hours, and there were no objections to Heydrich's words: on the contrary, several participants made their own contributions, notably as regards the fate of half-Jews, or calling for priority to be given to evacuating Jews from the "General Government".

At the end of the conference, Heydrich was clearly satisfied. According to Eichmann's testimony at his trial, this was the first time he had ever seen Heydrich so relaxed, chatting with Müller, smoking a cigarette and drinking a glass of cognac, something he had never done before.

Following this conference, Operation *Reinhard was* launched, the systematic elimination of all Jews in Poland and European Russia.

In a speech to SS and SD officials in Paris in May 1942, Heydrich declared that "the death sentence had been pronounced for all the Jews of Europe". According to historian Eberhard Jäckel, "the supreme architect of the genocide was not Himmler, but Heydrich. He pushed Hitler himself".

Heydrich was also active in the Nazi persecution of Gypsies. On March 1, 1938, he issued the decrees implementing the decree of December 8, 1937, organizing racial segregation of Gypsies, and in particular prohibiting mixed marriages. In October and November 1939, he helped prepare the expulsion of Gypsies from the Reich, which he organized in April 1940.

An aviator in search of glory

His activities as head of the SD and his promotions within the SS were not enough to satisfy Heydrich's need for glory: he also wanted to be a war hero.

In 1939, he was trained as a fighter pilot and took part in engagements over Poland, Norway and the Netherlands. Without a single victory to his credit, he capsized on take-off in May 1940 and damaged his aircraft when it was rolled into a hangar in 1941: these blunders were transformed into exploits by propaganda.

Despite Himmler's formal prohibition, it flew again during the invasion of the Soviet Union. On June 22, 1941, it was shot down by anti-aircraft defenses and crash-landed behind enemy lines. The panic was total: the head of the RSHA, Himmler's closest deputy, was in danger of falling into Soviet hands. But he is quickly rescued by members of Einsatzgruppe D and escapes capture.

This poor flying career, with no air combat victories, nevertheless earned him the Iron Cross First Class. After this incident, Himmler put a definitive end to Heydrich's career as an aviator.

Vice-Governor of Bohemia-Moravia

From 1931 onwards, Heydrich's career followed in Himmler's footsteps: at the head of the SD and then the RSHA, Heydrich purged the party, hunted down opponents, organized the Einsatzgruppen and put in place the mechanisms for the destruction of Europe's Jews. In 1941, it took a new course.

On September 24, 1941, Hitler appointed Heydrich "deputy" (German: *stellvertretender*) to the Governor of the Protectorate of Bohemia-Moravia, Konstantin von Neurath. Neurath, aged 68, was judged to be ineffective and was officially placed on sick leave. While Neurath officially remained in place, he no longer had a say in the matter, and the situation was clear to everyone: Heydrich became "number one" in Bohemia-Moravia. On the same day, he was promoted to SS-Obergruppenführer *und General der Polizei*.

A significant extension of his powers, this appointment also gave Heydrich direct access to the highest leaders of the Third Reich, without having to go through Himmler. What's more, he was convinced it would give him a more statesmanlike profile.

In this way, he capitalized on his successes and made people forget his failures, such as the trumped-up charge of homosexuality brought against General Werner von Fritsch, which led to Fritsch's acquittal by the Reich War Tribunal on March 17, 1938.

Upon his arrival in Prague, Heydrich had Prime Minister Alois Eliáš, who had been in contact with the Czechoslovak government in exile in London, arrested and sentenced to death. He brought the president of the puppet government, Hácha, to heel, in order to dispel even the slightest hint of independence from the Reich.

As the Czechoslovakian population was not sufficiently docile, Heydrich quickly used his weapon of choice: terror.

Between September 27, the date of his arrival, and November 29, four hundred Czechoslovakians were executed. The Gestapo took up residence in the Petschek Palace and disappeared over four thousand opponents and resistance fighters. Heydrich also set about emptying the Protectorate of its Jewish population, deporting them to the Theresienstadt concentration camp, then to the extermination camps.

He also wanted to maintain Czechoslovakian industrial production, vital to the German war effort, and no longer appear solely as an executioner. He increased food rations, set up soup kitchens and fought against the black market.

His responsibilities in the Protectorate did not prevent Heydrich from continuing to run the RSHA, at the cost of constant travel back and forth between Prague and Berlin. In particular, he ensured that the Anglophile tendencies of some German youth, who appreciated swing music, were suppressed. He also closely monitored the recruitment of prostitutes for *Salon Kitty*, a luxury brothel frequented by many celebrities, whose rooms were rigged with microphones, without any convincing results.

After just a few months of absolute rule over the Protectorate of Bohemia-Moravia, Heydrich knew he was feared. He also believed he was respected, even appreciated, by the "healthy part" of the population.

Heydrich's death

On the morning of May 27, 1942, Heydrich was at the height of his power: *SS-Obergruppenführer* and "vice-governor" - but *de facto* "governor" - of Bohemia-Moravia for eight months, director of the RSHA, decorated on numerous occasions, recognized by the most senior figures in the Reich, including Hitler himself, he planned to transpose to France the methods he had implemented in Prague.

For him, the future holds great promise and, at just 38, he is determined to continue his ascent.

The ambush of May 27, 1942

On May 27, 1942, at around 10:35 a.m., without any particular escort or protection, sitting next to the driver in the front seat of a convertible convertible, Heydrich made his usual twenty-kilometer journey from his residence in Panenské Břežany to the Černín palace (Czech: *Černínský palác*), where his offices were located on the Hradčany hill.

On this route, three Czechoslovak resistance fighters, all parachuted in on the night of December 28-29, 1941 from England, were ambushed: Slovak Jozef Gabčík and Czech

Jan Kubiš of the *Anthropoid* group, and Czech Josef Valčík of the *Silver A* group.

Gabčík and Kubiš wait at a streetcar stop on a sharp hairpin bend near Bulovka Hospital in Prague's 8-Libeň district. They are waiting to be warned by the third man, Valčík, stationed a hundred meters upstream, who is acting as a lookout.

Valčik signals the arrival of Heydrich's Mercedes with a mirror. When the car, idling on the bend, passes within three meters of Gabčík, he rushes in front of it to stop it and aims his Sten at Heydrich, but the weapon jams and no shot goes off. Heydrich orders his driver to stop the car and, as he stands up to try to shoot Gabčík, the third member of the commando, Kubiš, who is now at the rear of the car throws a modified anti-tank grenade, which explodes near the right rear wheel. Between the rear fender and the door, the bodywork is pierced by shrapnel: metal debris and fragments of seat fiber are thrown out and penetrate Heydrich's back.

After an exchange of pistol fire, the driver, *SS-Oberscharführer* Johannes Klein, sets off in pursuit of Kubiš, who rides a bicycle and flees behind the immobilized car. Heydrich, apparently not feeling his wounds, also gets out of the car, but staggers back and tries to chase Gabčík, who has left in front of the car: he promptly collapses on the ground. Klein fails to catch up with Kubiš and returns to Heydrich; the latter is bleeding profusely and orders Klein to pursue Gabčík on foot. Klein dashes off again and finds Gabčík in a butcher's store, but the parachutist fires his pistol twice, seriously wounding Klein in the leg, allowing him to escape and reach a hideout, having taken a streetcar. At this point, the two fleeing paratroopers are convinced that their mission has failed.

It took an hour for Heydrich to be transported to the nearby Bulovka hospital in a delivery van. His wound was not fatal in itself, but the shrapnel from the bodywork had also penetrated the wound with particles of horsehair upholstery. He underwent an operation, made a gradual recovery and six days later was sitting up in bed having breakfast, but it was then that his condition suddenly worsened and he fell into a coma. The septicemia was devastating and rapidly generalized.

On June 4, 1942, at 9:24 a.m., Heydrich died at the age of 38.

Retaliation

On June 9, the men of the security police surrounded the village of Lidice, suspected of having sheltered the parachutists. The 184 men of the village were executed by the SS; the women were deported to Ravensbrück, from where a good proportion of them would return; by contrast, of the 105 children deported to Łódź, only 17 survived, the others having been gassed in Chełmno. Some of the village's children, with traits considered Aryan by the Nazis, were entrusted to German families, through the *Lebensborn*. After the massacre and deportations, Lidice was burnt down and razed to the ground.

Thanks to the local resistance network, Kubiš was smuggled into the crypt of the Church of Saints Cyril and Methodius in central Prague, soon followed by other members of the commandos parachuted in since December. Vladimir Petrek, the Orthodox priest, himself supplies the recluses with food and newspapers. Other members of the church were later informed of the presence of resistance fighters in the building.

The Germans are offering up to ten million crowns to anyone who can find the commando who murdered Heydrich.

Following the betrayal of a member of another commando - Karel Čurda, of the *Out Distance* commando *(en)* parachuted on March 28, 1942 - who gave, among other things, the name of the Moravec family who had sheltered the parachutists before the attack, and after "extensive" interrogation of this family, the Germans managed to locate the commando hidden in the church along with the other parachutists.

The real reasons for Čurda's betrayal are still unknown today.

On June 18, at 4:15 a.m., the church was surrounded by 800 soldiers, tasked with capturing the parachutists alive, as the Germans wished at all costs to organize a trial "to set an example" commensurate with the importance of the victim. A veritable siege battle ensued, to which the members of the commando put up fierce resistance. After the besiegers attempted to flood the crypt, the seven resistance fighters finally perished in the fighting, or were wounded and then killed themselves, after having considered escaping through the drains by digging a hole in the crypt wall. After the fighting, the traitor Čurda is put in charge of identifying the bodies of the resistance fighters lined up in front of the church. The Gestapo cut off the heads of the corpses and displayed them on a shelf, before which they then paraded relatives and friends.

Repression continued throughout the summer of 1942, claiming over a thousand victims. In Lezaky, the men and women of the village - a total of 33 people - were all shot on June 24 after the discovery of a clandestine transmitter. The accomplices and sympathizers of the commando members were sentenced to death. The Orthodox bishop of Prague, M Gordaz, the priest of the church in which the parachutists had taken refuge,

Vladimir Petrek, and two other clerics were executed after a trial on September 1. Two hundred and thirty-six other condemned prisoners were deported to Mauthausen and liquidated on October 24.

Funerals and inheritance

Repatriated to Berlin, Heydrich's body was given a state funeral on June 9, 1942, at the Invalides cemetery, orchestrated with Nazi pomp and circumstance. Heinrich Himmler, *Reichsführer-SS*, began by praising "the rare purity of the deceased [who] from the depths of his soul and blood, understood, realized and materialized Adolf Hitler's conception of the world".

After Himmler, it was the Führer himself, Adolf Hitler, who paid tribute to the deceased: "I have few words to dedicate to this dead man. He was one of the best National Socialists, one of the staunchest defenders of the German Reich idea, and one of the most resolute opponents of all the enemies of the Reich" (Adolf Hitler, June 9, 1942).

In private, Hitler railed against Heydrich's recklessness: "Heroic gestures like driving around in an open car [...] are follies the nation did not need. Men of Heydrich's political stature should be aware that they are being watched like game, and that countless people have only one idea in mind: how to kill them...".

Ernst Kaltenbrunner took over the reins of the RSHA on January 30, 1943, after a period of interim management by Himmler, but failed to achieve his predecessor's level of power and influence.

From May 1942 to April 1945, Lina Heydrich lived in the castle and estate of Jungfer-Breschnan, near Prague, which she had maintained by prisoners taken from the Theresienstadt concentration camp. It was in the castle grounds that, in the presence of Heinrich Himmler, she had her son Klaus, who had been accidentally hit by a van on October 24, 1943, buried.

During the flight from Soviet troops, she requisitioned the services of the bus driver involved in her son's fatal accident, who the Gestapo had claimed had no responsibility for Klaus's death: he disappeared during the journey.

Prosecuted and convicted during the denazification process in Germany, Lina Heydrich multiplied her proceedings before finally being exonerated; she then brought suit after suit and finally obtained a pension on the basis of a judgment declaring Reinhard Heydrich to have been the victim of an act of war. After defending her husband's memory in the press and in her memoirs, going so far as to assert repeatedly that he had had no part in the extermination of the Jews, she died on her native island on August 14, 1985.

The man with the iron heart

Tall (1.85 meters), blond, athletic, a sportsman and, in particular, a world-class fencer, a fine violinist, married to a convinced Nazi and father of four children, with real physical courage, Heydrich seems, in many respects, to fit the profile of the *Übermensch*. But he was also a fickle husband, an inveterate womanizer, a fan of ethylic parties into which he dragged his colleagues, a naval officer with a frail voice and a short-lived career, an inexperienced fighter pilot with no victories to his credit.

One of the most striking features of Heydrich's personality is his total inability to show, or even feel, the slightest sentiment, apart from contempt, particularly towards his deputies, or through his frequent and terrible fits of anger. For all those who came into contact with him, whether accomplices or victims, he was a cold, hard man, one of the most feared of the Nazi regime.

For Albert Speer, "Heydrich was a cold man who always controlled himself and formulated his ideas with the rigor of an intellectual"; for Walter Schellenberg, "he could be incorrect to the point of cruelty. [...] This did not prevent him, given that his superior, Reichsführer-SS Himmler, attached great importance to the image of family life, from playing the role of tender husband and good father [...]"; speaking of Heydrich, Ernst Kaltenbrunner declared during his imprisonment at the Nuremberg trials: "He was a terribly ambitious man with a thirst for power. This desire for power was without measure, and he was extraordinarily intelligent and astute"; according to historian Joachim Fest, "he was a man like a whip, in his Luciferian coldness of feeling, his quiet amorality and his inextinguishable thirst for power".

For historian Robert Gerwarth, there have been two successive images of Heydrich in historiography and popular literature. The first is that of the perverse, diabolical Nazi. It has its origins in the testimonies of former Nazis, often Heydrich's subordinates anxious to protect themselves: Werner Best, Karl Wolff and Walter Schellenberg. It is propagated by popular works such as Charles Wighton's. Mixed in with this is the allegation of Heydrich's Jewish parentage, repeated after the war by former SS men like Wilhelm Höttl and Himmler's former masseur Felix Kersten. It has been taken up by a number of historians, most notably Joachim Fest. The second image of Heydrich, on the other hand, shows a cold, bureaucratic technocrat, more careerist than ideologue, following the thesis put forward by Hannah Arendt during the Eichmann trial. This approach has been taken up by Günther Deschner in particular.

Hard-working, a good organizer, able to surround himself with efficient deputies despite their diverse backgrounds, he demonstrated great determination and ambition. Demanding of his colleagues, inaccessible to doubt or criticism, he showed total obedience to his immediate superior, Heinrich Himmler.

In popular culture

Novels

- Laurent Binet, *HHhH* ["*Himmlers Hirn heißt Heydrich*" in French: "Himmler's brain is called Heydrich"], Paris, Le Livre de Poche, coll. "Littérature & Documents", May 4, 2011, 2 ed. (1 ed. 2010 with Grasset), 448 pp. (ISBN 978-2253157342).
- Paul Greveillac, *L'étau*, Paris, Gallimard, coll. "Blanche", March 2022, 320 p. (ISBN 978-2-072-97315-4).

Cinematography

- 1943 :
  - Fritz Lang's *Les bourreaux meurent aussi (The Executioners Also Die)* focuses on the reprisals following the bombing, with Heydrich appearing briefly at the beginning, played by Hans Heinrich von Twardowski ;
  - Douglas Sirk's *Hitler's Madman* focuses more on the character of Heydrich, played by John Carradine.
- 1955: *Admiral Canaris*, released in 1955, played by Martin Held.

- 1964 : *Commando in Prague* (*Atentát*) by Jiří Sequens, a Czechoslovak film from 1964, recounts the rivalry between Canaris and Heydrich, the preparation of Czech agents in England, the contact with resistance fighters, the attack, the repression and finally the death of the agents in the church of Saints-Cyrillus-and-Methodius in Prague.
- 1975: *Seven Men at Dawn* directed by Lewis Gilbert, featuring a Heydrich played by Anton Diffring.
- 2001: *Conspiracy*, recounting the Wannsee Conference, the role of Heydrich is played by Shakespearean actor-director Kenneth Branagh.
- 2004: In Alexander Aravine's Russian film *The Red Orchestra*, released in 2004, his role is played by Sergei Garmash.
- 2011: Lidice, a Czech film, tells the story of Heydrich's assassination by the resistance and the Nazi massacre of the village of Lidice in retaliation.
- 2015: he appears in the series *The Master of the High Castle*, played by Ray Proscia.
- 2016 : *Anthropoid*, directed by Sean Ellis, details the resistance operation that led to Heydrich's death.

- 2017: *HHhH*, adapted from the novel of the same name by Laurent Binet, tells the story of Heydrich's rise and assassination. It stars Jason Clarke.
- 2022 : The Conference, a German historical drama re-enacting the Wannsee Conference. Heydrich is played by Austrian actor Philipp Hochmair.

Other books by United Library

https://campsite.bio/unitedlibrary

Milton Keynes UK
Ingram Content Group UK Ltd.
UKHW020938220424
441551UK00019B/1421